A is for Axel

An Ice Skating Alphabet

Written by Kurt Browning and Illustrated by Melanie Rose

Back cover photo by Kimberley Stickel.

Sleeping Bear Press and Kurt Browning would like to acknowledge and thank Karen Cover, visitor services coordinator of the World Figure Skating Museum & Hall of Fame.

Sleeping Bear Press™

310 North Main Street, Suite 300
Chelsea, MI 48118
www.sleepingbearpress.com

THOMSON

GALE

© 2006 Thomson Gale, a part of the Thomson Corporation.

Thomson, Star Logo and Sleeping Bear Press are trademarks and Gale is a registered trademark used herein under license.

Printed and bound in Canada.

10 9 8 7 6 5 4 3 2 1

Library of Congress Cataloging-in-Publication Data

Browning, Kurt.
A is for axel : an ice skating alphabet / written by Kurt Browning ; illustrated by Melanie Rose.
p. cm.
ISBN 1-58536-280-8
1. Skating—Juvenile literature. 2. Alphabet books. I. Rose, Melanie, ill. II. Title.

GV850.223.B76 2005
796.91—dc22   2005027790

To everyone who keeps me young,
especially Sonita and Gabe

KURT

❊

For my mum—
a fanatical figure skating fan

MELANIE

The Axel jump is named after Norwegian Axel Paulsen. Paulsen first completed the jump in 1882 rumored to be wearing a pair of speed skates. The Axel is traditionally thought of as one of the most difficult of all the jumps because of the forward take-off and the extra half revolution it takes to land backward. The skater almost always goes into the Axel backward and then steps forward on the outside of the blades' edge and throws both his arms and the free leg forward into the air. There are single, double, and triple versions of the Axel.

When a young skater lands his first Axel jump it is always a day he will remember. In 1978 Canadian Vern Taylor landed the first triple Axel in competition at the World Championships in Ottawa, Ontario. Brian Orser, nicknamed "Mr. Triple Axel," became known as the king of the triple Axel and for many years was the only one in the world who had truly mastered the big jump.

A is for Axel jump.
It's difficult but fun.
What a big day in a skater's life,
when they land their first one.

An extra half turn
makes the Axel the best,
and it's why this jump
is harder than the rest.

B is for Boot,
  and B is for Blade.
    Put them together
and a skate is made.

The proper fit, or how the boot sits on the skater's foot, is important at every level. For the first few years of skating, support and comfort are key factors. A plastic molded skate can offer the support needed, but also the comfort of soft padding. These skates come out of the box ready for the ice. Learning how to skate is more enjoyable if your feet are warm and comfortable.

As the skill of a figure skater grows and changes, he or she sometimes considers leather boots instead of plastic. For advanced skaters, boots and blades are sold separately. This gives skaters the ability to match the boot they like with the blade they want.

Boots can be made of fuzzy leather called suede or hard shiny leather. Also, skates come in more colors than just black and white so if purple is your favourite color, then purple's great while you skate.

C is for the Coaches
who teach you so much.
They'll give your skating
their personal touch.

From singles to doubles
then triples you grow,
with coaches beside you
sharing all that they know.

Just as in other sports, skating coaches are important. From little children learning to skate in group lessons to Olympic champions, almost every skater has at least one coach. Beginner skaters usually work in groups with other children and one or two coaches. As skills improve, individual coaches and private lessons are available.

Each coach has her own style of teaching and her own way to teach jumps and spins. Most figure skating coaches were at one time skaters themselves. Sometimes it takes some time to find a good match between coach and skater. Coaches know that having proper technique as a young skater is important to learning safe jumps and spins. It is only after their student is strong enough and consistent with a move that they go on to the next level. Coaches also work on a skater's posture and body position as well as conditioning, stretching, and strength.

It is very important for skaters to have confidence in their coaches, and for coaches to believe in their skaters.

Music makes it natural for a skater to want to dance, but the dance event at a skating competition requires not only music but also a partner! What makes dancing difficult is that two skaters must skate very close to each other and know where the other is at all times. The skates that dancers use have less support and are cut shorter on the ankle so dancers can point their toes more. Since dancer's steps are very close to their partner's steps, the tail of the blade is shorter to help prevent tripping one another.

The first World Championships in ice dancing were in 1952 and held at the World Figure Skating Championships in Paris, yet it did not become an Olympic medal sport until 1976.

Unlike the pairs event, in dance the man cannot lift the woman any higher than his shoulder and jumps cannot have more than one rotation. There are many set dances that skaters can learn. For example, the waltz and the canasta move around the ice in a set pattern. One of the hardest dances is the tango because it involves changing positions with sharp, quick movements. After many years of practice, dancers can perform any style of dance together.

The free dance competition is very exciting because couples choose their own style of movement and music and can choreograph any steps they choose for their program.

Dd

D is for Dancing—
boy and girl together,
moving across the ice
as light as a feather.

Hand in hand,
they dance as one
with turns and twizzles
'til the music's done.

E is for Edge.
It's easily seen—
a skater makes one
when he's on a lean.

Forward or backward
and there when you swerve,
inside or out,
and always on a curve.

E e

Edges in figure skating can mean two different things. A skate's blade is much wider than a knife's blade and there are two very separate sides or edges. The side that is on the "inside" of the foot is called the inside edge. The one on the outside of the blade is of course called the outside edge. These two edges are used to steer the blade.

Another meaning for the word edge is not quite as literal as the actual edge of the blade, but more about what the skater looks like while using that edge. A great skater can use edges to lean into a corner or curve on a very deep angle. The momentum and the edge biting into the ice hold the skater up. When a skater can change direction quickly while maintaining a lean, you could say that this skater has "good edges."

F is for a skating Fall.
You might go down if you slip.
Beginners or world champions—
anyone can trip!

Many might agree that falling down while ice-skating needs no explanation. However, learning how to be prepared in case of a fall and how to get back on your skates is one of the first lessons for young skaters. For safety, beginners often wear helmets and sometimes wrist guards. These are important pieces of equipment to wear while mastering basic elements of skating. Some coaches use a harness system that the skater wears around his waist. While tied to a pulley system from the ceiling, the coach controls the skater as he practices a new jump

Skaters can actually learn how to react so that they have less of a chance of getting hurt while falling. Also, instructors work with young children, teaching them how to get back up on their feet after a fall. Getting up is easiest while on your hands and knees. Bring one foot up on the blade, put your hands on your knee and push up from there. Like skiing, skating is a sport where falling down is a part of the learning process. Once you start learning single, double, and especially triple jumps you might wear padding on your bum. Falling is simply a part of skating and even the very best in the world fall down sometimes.

Ff

Gg

An effortless glide across the ice is one of the greatest feelings while on skates. After building up speed or momentum a skater can carry that speed over the ice a great distance without pushing. A few typical positions that might be held while gliding are the spiral and the spread eagle. American Janet Lynn, who began skating before she was three years old, is known for how effortlessly she used her glide. Yuka Sato, who won the 1994 World Championships in her home country of Japan, is a now a professional skater who glides so smoothly that her skates are practically silent on the ice.

A better "glide" is achieved by using the blades in perfect alignment with the direction the skater is going. If there is no skidding or drag of the toe picks, a smoother glide is achieved. There are many things that can slow down the glide: improper sharpening, nicks or rust on the bottom of the blade, or bad alignment of the blade to the boot.

Perhaps the worst thing that can prevent a skater from gliding is, of course, forgetting to take the guards off the blades before stepping on the ice. The condition of a skater's blades is very important and could have an impact on the skater's ability to perform. Wearing guards on your blades while off the ice will make the sharpening, and even the blades, last longer.

An amazing thing about skating
is the ability to Glide.
Just get up some good speed,
and then enjoy the ride.

But if you want to try it,
you should take this advice.
Take off your guards
or you will hit the ice.

Jackson Haines is known as the Father of Modern Figure Skating bringing dance and theatrics to the sport. Haines was the U.S. Men's Champion in 1865.

Another **H** in history is Sonja Henie. Sonja competed in the 1924 Olympics when she was just 11 years old. She won the world's figure-skating crown ten consecutive years, the European title eight times in a row, and the Olympic figure-skating championships in 1928, 1932, and 1936. After her last Olympic win she moved to the United States, turned professional, and became a skating movie star.

An outstanding athlete, American skater Dick Button was a five-time world champion (1948-1952) and two-time Olympic gold medallist (1948 and 1952).

Scott Hamilton is a four-time world champion (1981-84) and won Olympic gold in 1984. Scott is known for his back flips and the excitement they give the audience.

Dorothy Hamill, along with Scott, is credited with bringing popularity to professional ice-skating shows. Dorothy also skated her way to becoming a National, World, and Olympic Champion with training from Carlo Fassi, who had also coached champion Peggy Fleming. During the 1976 Olympics Dorothy's pixie hairstyle was copied by millions of girls worldwide.

H is for the History—
so many moments to report.
Most important of all
are the skaters in the sport.

The quality of the ice is most important. Even the best skaters in the world have trouble on ice that is bumpy, too hard, or too soft. Ice that is very hard can become brittle and will shatter when a skater lands a jump or uses her toe pick for a take off. Sometimes the edge of the blade slips away on hard ice, while on very soft ice it holds too well making turning difficult and dangerous. Hot water is used while making or flooding the ice, filling all the cuts and holes while melting it all just enough to make it smooth like glass. Every touch of the blade to newly flooded ice can be seen like a sketch on the surface.

Important skating competitions, even the Olympics, have been held on outdoor rinks. Unlike modern arenas, the ice was never perfect with bumps, frost, or even snow. Sometimes, if competing on a windy day, skaters would change the directions of the jumps to avoid fighting against the wind and even to possibly take advantage of it.

A lake or stream can freeze perfectly flat if the conditions are just right. Skating outdoors is a special treat for people who enjoy skating and many first learn to skate on backyard rinks.

I i

Dad pushed off all the snow
    to reveal smooth, beautiful Ice.
With my skates and my friends
        there's nothing quite as nice.

A grand arena is very warm
with no bumps or cracks to see,
        but shiny outdoor ice
    is the perfect kind for me.

J is for Jumping
        high into the air,
flying over the ice
        and landing with flair.

There are many reasons why people enjoy participating in or watching figure skating, but jumping would have to be close to the top on most people's list. Even if it's a girl's first bunny hop or a world class competitor's perfectly timed landing, jumping is fun. There are many different jumps to learn, and landing each one for the first time is always a good reason to celebrate.

Some jumps have different names depending on where you may live but here are some of the jumps in their generally accepted order of difficulty. The simple waltz jump or three jump is only half of a revolution from a forward takeoff. Next is the cherry flip or toe wally and it is usually the first full revolution jump a skater lands. The Salchow, named after Sweden's Ulrich Salchow, is an edge-jump, as is the loop. The flip is next and then the Lutz. The Lutz is named for Alois Lutz and these are called toe jumps because the toe pick assists the skater into the air. The Axel is an edge jump like the Salchow and loop.

In the history of skating many men have been known for their great jumping: Brian Boitano, Brian Orser, Ilia Kulik, and "Jumping Joe" Sabovick, to name a few. But possibly the most powerful and exciting jumper in the sport was a woman. Japan's Midori Ito was the first woman to ever land a triple Axel (1989 World Championships) and often outjumped everyone in the competition, including competitors in the men's event.

When you watch a group of figure skaters zoom and whiz over the ice, it might make you wonder how they don't bump into each other more often. Safety is most important, and being aware of what you, as well as what everybody else is doing at all times, helps to avoid collisions. Skating with your head down, or not paying attention is dangerous as many skaters can get to some high speeds. A colorful scarf around the waist or a bright vest is sometimes worn by the one skater who is skating to his music at the time and so has the right of way. Being respectful to your fellow skaters, teammates, and competitors as well as coaches and judges shows good sportsmanship. Respecting the ice itself is also important.

Learning a new jump can be frustrating but kicking the ice in anger, as well as rude, is dangerous. The hole left in the ice makes it easy to trip into. How you act on the ice is at least as important as how you skate. If you get frustrated, take your energy out on a few high-flying hitch kicks instead.

K is for Kick,
    and it isn't very nice
if a skater gets mad
    and then kicks the ice.

But there is another kind.
    It's called a hitch kick—
    a high-flying move
        and a really cool trick.

L₁

L is for Laces,
that hold our skates tight.
Sometimes we need help
to make them feel right.

The laces in a figure skate do much more than just hold the skate on your foot. By tying up the laces you are closing the boot around your ankle, which gives you the support you need. Giving support to the ankle is one of the skate's most important jobs. Over time, each skater finds his own way to lace up his skates to suit his skating style.

Tying laces on a figure skate is a little different than tying tennis or running shoes and even different than tying hockey skate laces. Most figure skates have what are called "hooks" that run up the ankle of the boot. With four or five hooks on each side it allows the skate to open up farther, which makes it easier to get your foot in and out. Using hooks rather than eyelets also makes it faster to tie up skates. It takes some strength to properly tie up a skate and is why children often need help putting their skates on. Not only is it very difficult to skate properly in boots that have been tied too loosely, but you could also twist your ankle.

M is for the Music—
maybe soft, maybe bold?
Make the right choice for you,
and your medal may be gold.

Figure skating is one of the few sports that uses music within the competitive event. It is the skaters' relationship and interaction with their musical choice that brings the artistic element to the sport.

A good match between the skater and her music engages the audience and the judges. In competition there are rules such as how long a solo may be, and no lyrics or phrases may be part of the skater's music.

Often the coach chooses the music for her students. Knowledge of music and a skater's unique style are important for a coach to know. Some skaters use a choreographer, a person who arranges the movements that make up a solo. After the choice is made and the music is edited to the correct length, the choreographer helps make up the program. How skaters move to the music is called their choreography and it is very important to the artistic mark, which is based on the performance to the music, ice coverage, and general flow.

N is for Needs more practice
your coach will say.
And Never give up
day after day.

The sport of figure skating is a difficult one. Improving each day means dedication and long hours of practice. **N** is also for "never forget safety." Figure skating is a fluid and graceful sport, but that does not mean that there are not some dangers that go along with it. Never forget your helmet when you are learning how to skate. This is an important piece of equipment to wear until you master the basic elements of skating. Depending on what a skater is practicing, elbow pads, wrist guards, or even bum pads may be worn.

Another way to stay safe and free from injury is to warm up your body before stepping on the ice. This is especially important but more so when the arena is cold. Once off the ice, skaters should stretch to prevent stiffness. This helps the body to recover so that you are ready to skate again the next day.

N
n

Many dream of a place on the Olympic podium, and that will become reality for only a select few. Figure skating competition in the Olympic Games is held every four years. Athletes from around the world work very hard for the chance to represent their home country, to walk behind their flag at the opening ceremony, and to compete against the best in the world. Figure skating is consistently one of, if not the most, watched events on television during the Olympics.

The Olympic Games include the Summer Olympics with sports such as running and swimming and cold weather events such as skiing, hockey, and figure skating events that are part of the Winter Olympics.

Actually, figure skating began as an Olympic event at the summer games in 1908 before being held during the first offical Winter Olympic Games in 1924. These early Olympics had men's, women's, and pairs events only. Ice dancing was added as an Olympic sport in 1976.

For many skaters around the world the **O**lympics is a dream.
If they become their country's champion,
they'll be on the Olympic team.

They have to work for many years,
for a chance to represent their nation.
To perhaps stand atop the podium,
with flowers and a standing ovation.

P is for a "perfect" Pairs program
where two skaters are a team.
It takes extra time and practice,
to achieve that perfect dream.

P is for the Pairs team
that keeps you on your toes.
A pair performance is exciting,
with all the lifts and throws.

Pair skaters are known for big lifts and throws but they can also perform some very dramatic spins in pair positions. Pair skaters actually perform spins in two different ways—"side-by-side" which are done individually (although ideally in unison), and "pair spins," in which the skaters are touching while they spin together.

A pair team, unlike a dance team, is allowed to take lifts up and over the head of the man. Once in the air, it gets even more exciting as the woman changes positions while they speed across the ice before he puts her down. When the man assists the woman with her jumps, she can fly across the ice much farther than any skater could ever do on her own. Pair skaters are known for big lifts and throws, but they can also perform some very dramatic spins in pair positions.

When pair skaters perform jumps, skaters should take off and land at the same time; both should have the same number of revolutions, similar height and distance, and similar landing positions. Having another person as your pair partner not only gives opportunities for lifts, throws, and pair spins but also special moves you can do only with a partner.

The quad jump is the most difficult jump in the sport of figure skating and at one time only a very select few could perform the leap. Canadian Kurt Browning gets credit for landing the first quad jump ever—during the 1988 world championships in Budapest, Hungary.

Even though a completed quadruple takes less than a second to complete, it looks much bigger and is more impressive than a three-revolution jump. If a skater could actually spin for one full minute, he would complete almost 300 revolutions.

Canadian Elvis Stojko became the first figure skater to use the quadruple jump in combination with a double jump and was also the first person to land a quadruple-triple combination.

Timothy Gobel of the United States is the first person to ever land three quads in one competitive routine. The more turns a skater completes while jumping, the less room for error. The athletic strength, the skater's determination, and his guts make the quadruple jump exciting and a very well-respected feat.

Q is for a Quad jump
        with four turns in the air.
If someday you land one,
            everyone will stare.

The rink becomes a blur,
your spinning now don't quit.
        The most exciting jump in the world,
            and you just landed it.

R r

Maybe it's the ability to rotate that changes a casual skate across the ice into figure skating. It takes years and years of practice to turn a simple two-foot spin into a spin so fast that it actually begins to look blurred to the viewer.

Rotation is started while entering a spin on the ice or a jump in the air. Once started, the rotation is increased by pulling the legs and arms in close to the body. Stopping this rotation is accomplished by opening up again, and it's called "checking" the rotation.

There are three basic spinning positions: sit, camel, and upright. With variations and combinations of these three spins, all the other spins are formed. For example, the flying sit spin, the Hamill Camel (after Dorothy), and the Beilman.

The camel spin resembles a spinning spiral and when Dorothy Hamill perfected her own way to switch from a camel to a sit spin the variation was named for her. Similarly, using her talent and flexibility, Switzerland's Denise Beilman was able to create a spin so unusual that it simply had to be named for her.

And, yes, skaters do get dizzy, but with practice they get used to it.

R is for Rotating.
It makes you look quite busy.
Either in the air or on the ice,
it can make you very dizzy.

Skating rinks can be cold, so dressing warmly is a good idea. Mittens and a sweater, maybe with your badges down the sleeve, will keep you warm when you practice, but what about the big test or competition?

After choosing the music and creating the chorography there is still one thing left to do, besides practice. Skaters need outfits to pull all of the elements together for the performance. Figure skaters are athletes, but they are in many ways artists as well. Having a costume or outfit that suits their style and music choice makes the audience appreciate their performance even more.

Judges are especially influenced by the choice of outfit because they are watching to see how well the skater will be interpreting their music choice. For example, it would be confusing to watch a skater who is wearing a tuxedo while skating to western music. Sometimes it is a family member like Mom or a friend who sews the outfit. Other times it can simply be bought ready to skate from a store, but the skaters you see on television usually get their outfits from professional designers. An outfit should not only look great and suit the music style but also allow the skater to be able to move freely and feel comfortable while she performs. It should make the skater feel fantastic, just like that special sweater did when she was young.

S is for so many things,
        like your special skating Sweater.
    And S is for all the Sequins
            that make your sweater better.

Tt

T is for Turning, Turning,
this way and that.
Be careful how you turn
so you don't go splat!

Turning in your footwork.
Turning on your toe.
Turning your trusting partner
around and to and fro.

For recreational skaters, turning is really all about having fun. Changing direction from frontward to backward or trying a quick turn with some speed is exciting and challenging. If you are trying to pass a test or are in a competition, then all types of turning become very important.

The ability to turn in one direction and then back in the other on either foot, all while travelling at different speeds are some of the elements judges look for in good footwork. Most turns are done on the middle part of the blade, but great skating includes turns on both the toe and the heel as well.

Depending on which side or edge of the blade you start the turn on, and which edge you end the turn on decides which particular turn you just did. These turns all have names such as rockers, counters, brackets, and three turns. Including them all in your program shows a variety of turning ability.

If you turn a skate blade over and look down the length of the blade you will see a U shape along it. It is that U shape that gives each side of the blade the edge it needs to hold onto the ice. If your skate's blade is flat, the edges will be dull and you should use caution when you skate. A special flat, spinning stone sends sparks into the air while it sharpens the blade. How deep the groove, or how deep the "U" will decide how sharp the blade will be.

Taking care of your blades helps give you the best conditions possible for skating. Blades should be dried after every session to prevent them from rusting. Rubber guards are put over blades while walking and soft ones are used when skates are stored to keep the nicks away.

Equipment has advanced since ancient times when blades were actually bones strapped to a boot. Archaeologists in Sweden have found ancient skate blades made of elk, horse, and reindeer bones—at least they didn't rust. Later, wood and metal replaced bone when crafting skate blades.

U
u

Look and see the shape of a U
underneath your blade.
Turn your skate upside down to see
how left and right edges are made.

The two edges are kept sharp
with a flat spinning stone
but they didn't do these things,
back when blades were made of bone.

There are many little V's
on your blade's tip.
So when you jump with ease,
your pick won't slip.

The biggest difference between a hockey blade, a speed skating blade, and a figure skating blade is the toe pick, those shiny, pointy teeth at the front of the skate.

The toe picks are used to slow down by dragging them into the ice or they are used to jump into the air. Jumps in skating are usually divided into two groups: the edge jumps and the toe jumps. The toe pick is used in the takeoff of a toe jump, but it is also used to assist the skater into the air on the edge jumps as well. The pick is the last part of the blade to actually leave the ice.

The toe pick is also very important when landing jumps. If you watch a perfectly landed jump you will hardly notice the skater using the toe pick, but it is usually the very first part of the blade to touch the ice. As the landing continues, the pick helps grab into the ice. If the skater is leaning too far forward or even starting to fall the toe pick can actually help.

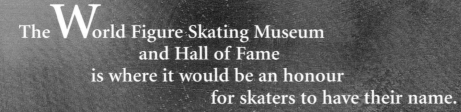

The World Figure Skating Museum and Hall of Fame is dedicated to preserving the worldwide history of figure skating and honouring outstanding participants in the sport. Located in Colorado Springs, Colorado, the Hall of Fame includes some of greatest names in figure skating: dancers Jayne Torvill and Christopher Dean, Dick Button, Scott Hamilton, Midori Ito, Sonja Henie, and Katarina Witt. To many, induction into the Hall of Fame is considered one of the highest honours a figure skater could ever achieve. Some members of the hall are also coaches or judges.

The museum is home to more than 3,500 video and film items dating as far back as Sonja Henie's 1928 Olympic winning performance. More than 20,000 skating pictures are part of the museum's collection, too.

The **W**orld Figure Skating Museum
and Hall of Fame
is where it would be an honour
for skaters to have their name.

W
W

Can you find the X
that this skater makes,
with each and every crossover
that this skater takes?

X is the score
you'll get for your skate
but even though you're done
the judges make you wait.

A crossover is when a skater lifts up one skate
and crosses it over the other while moving
forward or backward. This is the basic movement skaters use to build speed up on a circle
or a curve and it is easy to tell the level of any
skater just by watching his crossovers. Judges
watch for these stroking skills because they
show up in every aspect of skating and are
very important.

X also marks that unknown number the
judges will award the skater. The judges
take many things into consideration before
awarding the marks at a competition. What
spins and jumps the skater completed, how
difficult they were and how well they were
performed are a big part of the total score.
Other elements of the performance the judges
will be watching for are connecting steps
between elements, footwork sequences, music
interpretation, and chorography—just to name
a few. Each category receives a separate
score and while the skater and the audience
impatiently wait, scores are totaled. Sports
are always growing and changing. This means
the rules of that sport often have to change
as well. Figure skating no longer uses the
"perfect" score of 6.0 that existed for many
years. What has not changed is the traditional
award of gold, silver, and bronze medals to
the top three finishers.

Y y

Y is for You.
You're as proud as can be.
You have your own style
 as everyone can see.

You are you
and that's who you are.
 You are special—
  your own private star.

Perhaps figure skating is for you. Just like your voice, handwriting, or even your fingerprint is unique to you alone, your skating style is also all your own. The more you practice and the more you are influenced by the world around you, the more obvious your own style will become. And in figure skating, no one style is right or wrong. Skating gives each individual the chance to explore what she enjoys about the sport.

Skaters can be team players and join a precision team sharing the ice with 20 or more all moving in unison. Or you could be part of a smaller team of two people and dance or do pairs. Or just skate all by yourself.

Canadian Toller Cranston, 1976 Olympic bronze medallist and six-time Canadian champion, stood out from the rest of the competitors, partly by being himself. His hair was longer, his expression and artistry new, and his outfits were daring. He was an artist on and off the ice and his skating, like his paintings, showed his unique personality.

After a stunning performance or long hours of practice, a skater's countless zigs and zags appear as marks on the ice.

"Look, the Zamboni!" Skating is fun, but for some the Zamboni is a close second—a colourful, fun vehicle that can drive right on the ice and almost magically make the ice like new again. Frank Zamboni invented the motorized ice-resurfacing machine in 1949. Today there are other companies who also manufacture the machines.

As fun as it is to watch the machine on the ice, the Zamboni has a serious role to play. Only after all the skaters have cleared the ice does the resurfacing machine start its job. With spinning blades, the Zamboni actually shaves off the top layer of ice. The depth of the shavings depends on what the ice needs. The holes, bumps, or ruts that are in the ice are filled with a blanket of hot water that comes out of the back of the Zamboni. The Zamboni covers the entire ice surface, leaving a steaming, shiny sheet of ice ready and safe for the next bit of skating magic.

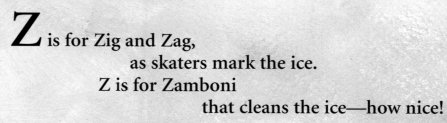

Z is for Zig and Zag,
      as skaters mark the ice.
   Z is for Zamboni
           that cleans the ice—how nice!

Kurt Browning

Known for his fluid movement and confidence on the ice, four-time world champion figure skater Kurt Browning spins, jumps, and glides his way through the alphabet with *A is for Axel: An Ice Skating Alphabet*. Kurt was the first figure skater to be named as Canada's outstanding male athlete, was honored by *Sports Illustrated* as one of the 50 greatest sports figures from Canada, and is a member of Canada's Sports Hall of Fame. Completing the first quadruple jump in competition earned Kurt his way into the *Guinness Book of Records*.

Kurt presently skates professionally with *Stars on Ice* and lives in Toronto with his wife and son.

Melanie Rose

Illustrator Melanie Rose's charming and lively oil paintings have graced the pages of several Sleeping Bear Press titles including *Z is for Zamboni: A Hockey Alphabet*; *H is for Homerun: A Baseball Alphabet*; and *M is for Maple: A Canadian Alphabet*. She makes her home in Mississauga, Canada, with her son Liam and their two cats, Mickey and Meesha.